Stenchford Plops
and the
Midnight Mega-Mufflerquakes

Luc Warmbath

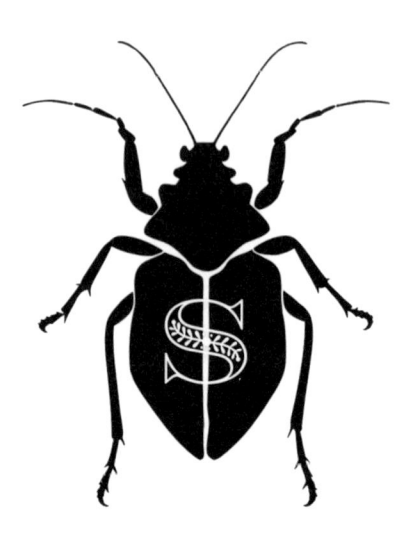

Copyright © 2024 by Luc Warmbath
All rights reserved.
No part of this publication may be reproduced, distributed, or transmitted in any form or by any means, including photocopying, recording, or other electronic or mechanical methods, without the prior written permission of the publisher, except as permitted by U.S. copyright law.
For permission requests, Email stinkbugpress@gmail.com
The story, all names, characters, and incidents portrayed in this production are fictitious. No identification with actual persons (living or deceased), places, buildings, and products is intended or should be inferred.
The character of Stenchford Plops
Book Cover by Luc Warmbath
Illustrations by Luc Warmbath
1st edition [2024] Stinkbug Press

In an old lemon tree on the outskirts of Crawlington lived Stenchford Plops, the stinkiest stink bug in town.

His claim to fame?

Epic farts—so powerful they could explode pies, wilt flowers, and send bugs scattering like it was the end of the world.

Stenchford had mastered the art of farting, turning his gas blasts into a fine, stinky art form.

Bugs from miles around would hold their noses, wipe their eyes, and laugh so hard they'd practically roll out of their shells.

Pong!

Wicked!

But one night, as Crawlington slept under the moon, something very strange happened.

PFFFT!

Prrrrrumble...
A thunderous rumble echoed through the streets. The whiffquake was so loud it rattled windows and sent sleepy bugs tumbling out of their beds.

The smell? Worse than a thousand rotten eggs baked in a car!

By morning, the town was buzzing with gossip and lingering stink.

"Did you hear that tooterboomer?" asked Honeydew the Bee, twitching her wings.

"Hear it? I thought my house was gonna explode!" said Sparky the Firefly, his wings still shaking.

"Stenchford cut the cheese!"

Everyone had the same idea:
It must've been Stenchford Plops!

"Stenchford! Cut it out with the midnight fart-o-thons!" Honeydew buzzed past his tree.

Stenchford scratched his head. "It wasn't me! Sure, I can blow the roof off with my farts, but that wasn't my stink!"

OH NO! Scentapocalypse!

But each night, at midnight—Pffft-BAM!—another massive **bootyquake** hit the town, rattling bug beds. Every morning, Stenchford faced stink-eye from all the bugs in Crawlington.

Stenchford protested, but no one believed him.

"Seriously, Stenchford? What gives?"

"I swear it's not me!"

I'm not letting everyone blame me for these Midnight Mega-**Mufflerquakes!**

Determined to clear his name, Stenchford decided to investigate.

That night, he stayed up late, perched on his tree like a fart detective. He was determined to sniff out the truth.

Yikes!

At midnight—Pffft-BAM!—another fart, a thunderbumble! so big it shook the trees. Stenchford's eyes widened. It's coming from the edge of town! he thought and zipped off, faster than a stink wave.

Stenchford zoomed through Crawlington and to the woods, following the stink trail.

Around a bend, he screeched to a stop, his wings flapping madly. In front of him was a dung beetle rolling a giant ball of poop the size of a watermelon.

The beetle let out a tiny Pfft!—then—KA-BOOM! A stink explosion knocked Stenchford back, making his eyes water.

A foulcano!

"Aha!" Stenchford cried, "It's you! You've been dropping these stink bombs every night!"

"I didn't mean to cause trouble! My name's Clodbert Smudge. I just moved to Crawlington, and when I get nervous... I fart."

The beetle nearly flipped over his poop ball in panic.

Stenchford blinked, antennas twitching. "You fart when you're nervous?"

Clodbert nodded, looking like he wanted to disappear into his poop ball. "Yeah, and it's so embarrassing. I didn't mean to stink up the whole town! I just get nervous rolling my poop ball, and... well... it just happens."

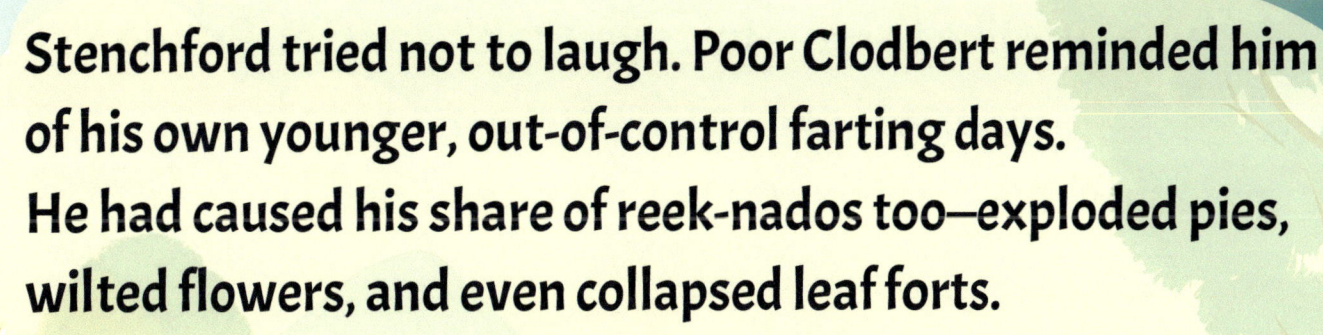

Stenchford tried not to laugh. Poor Clodbert reminded him of his own younger, out-of-control farting days.
He had caused his share of reek-nados too—exploded pies, wilted flowers, and even collapsed leaf forts.

He was secretly impressed. Clodbert had the power to stink like a swamp of rotting fish guts seasoned with skunk spray.

"Hey, it's cool," Stenchford said, grinning. "I know what it's like to have farts you can't control. But don't worry! I can teach you to manage it.

"You've just gotta learn when to hold it in and when to – well – let it rip!"

Clodbert's eyes widened. "You'd really help me? Even after all the trouble I caused?"

I smell trouble!

The next morning, Stenchford and Clodbert returned to town. Crawlington was already buzzing, but when they saw Stenchford, bugs gave him suspicious looks.

Stenchford cleared his throat. "Listen up! It wasn't me causing those stink bombs every night!" The crowd gasped.

Gawd Dang!

A dungfartle!

"Nope! The real culprit is my new friend here—Clodbert Smudge!" Stenchford nudged Clodbert forward.

"That's foul!"

Clodbert was shy and embarrassed "I'm really sorry. I didn't mean to stink up the whole town. I just get nervous and... well... fart."

stink bomb!

Silence. Then, Honeydew the Bee zoomed forward, buzzing so hard she nearly flipped. "Well, everyone farts but your stankbusters are epic!"

The crowd burst into laughter, and Stenchford's antennas perked up. "You're not alone, Clodbert. Here in Crawlington, we celebrate all kinds of talents—even the stinky ones."

You stink! And we love you!

From that day on, Stenchford and Clodbert became the best of farting buddies. They spent their days rolling poop balls, practicing fart control, and causing harmless stinky chaos that always ended in giggles.

You're the best Stenchford!

High five Clodbert!

Clodbert's farts were still powerful, but with Stenchford's help, they became more predictable.

Wow! The Grand Poobah himself!

Soon, Clodbert was known as "The Grand Poobah" and his farts became legendary. Crawlington was proud of its stinkiest duo.

One evening, as the bugs gathered for a picnic under the lemon tree, Clodbert let out a long, rumbling fart so powerful that it sent leaves flying like confetti.

Sploot!
Blorp!!

Bugs clung to their picnic blankets for dear life, their antennae flapping in the breeze of his gaseous explosion. Laughter erupted, and even a few beetles rolled onto their backs, giggling so hard they nearly passed out.

"Who cut the cheese!"

"Ripe!"

"See, Clodbert?" Stenchford chuckled. "Your farts are practically a weather event now!"

Clodbert grinned. "Thanks, Stenchford. You're a good friend."

"And you're the Grand Poobah!"

"My favorite smell is?"

And from that day forward, wherever Stenchford and Clodbert went, stink and laughter followed. Crawlington had never been stinkier—or happier.

THE END

Enjoyed the stink-filled adventure? Scan the QR code and share the fun—your words could inspire the next smelly adventure!
LOVE, STENCHFORD

Also from the mischievous mind of
Luc Warmbath

Stenchford Plops: The Stink Bug Who Lost His Fart
Luc Warmbath

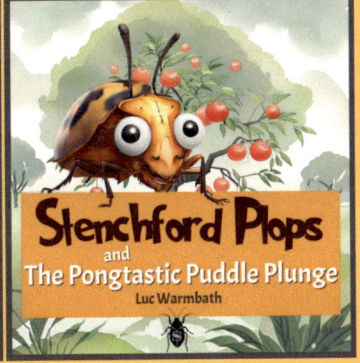

Stenchford Plops and The Pongtastic Puddle Plunge
Luc Warmbath

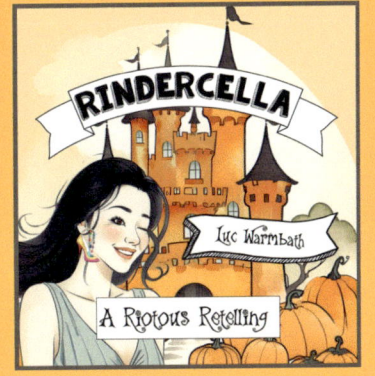

RINDERCELLA
Luc Warmbath
A Riotous Retelling

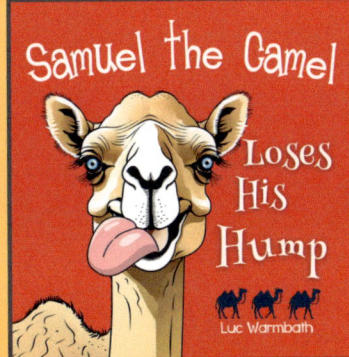

Samuel the Camel Loses His Hump
Luc Warmbath

Other titles in the Stenchford Plops series, turning stinky situations into hilarious adventures with life lessons that kids adore.

LIFE'S NO FAIRYTALE FOR RINDERCELLA

ONE HUMP, BIG HEART, ENDLESS ADVENTURE!

+Follow Luc Warmbath